Sacred Heart

Prayers & Devotions

"The Sacred Heart of Jesus,
pierced by our sins and for our salvation,
is quite rightly considered the chief sign and symbol of that…
love with which the divine Redeemer continually loves the eternal
Father and all human beings without exception."

(*Catechism of the Catholic Church* 478)

by
Donal Anthony Foley

All booklets are published thanks to the generous support of the members of the Catholic Truth Society

CATHOLIC TRUTH SOCIETY
PUBLISHERS TO THE HOLY SEE

Contents

 First published 2014 by The Incorporated Catholic Truth Society, 40-46 Harleyford Road London SE11 5AY Tel: 020 7640 0042 Fax: 020 7640 0046.

ISBN 978 1 86082 895 9

Origins and importance of the devotion

The wounding of Christ's heart on Calvary

The origins of the devotion to the Sacred Heart of Jesus go back to the origins of Christianity, to Christ's sacrificial death on the cross. In Chapter 19 of St John's Gospel, we read of what happened after the crucifixion, after Jesus' garments had been divided, after he had given Mary his mother to St John, and St John to her, and after he had cried out "I thirst," and then drunk the vinegar presented to him, before offering up his spirit to the heavenly father.

Then, while his dead body was on the cross, one of the soldiers pierced his side - his heart - with a spear, and blood and water gushed from the wound. St John pointed to the prophetic significance of this act, saying that it fulfilled the words of Zechariah, "They shall look on him whom they have pierced" (*Zc* 12:10).

The implication of this act of the soldier is that it showed that the very last drops of Christ's blood were shed for mankind, as a sign of his infinite love.

The importance of devotion to Christ's Sacred Heart

But even before this, during his public ministry, Christ had referred to this love of his for mankind, of his gentle and lowly heart, and invited all to share this love: "Come to me, all you who labour and are heavy laden, and I will give you rest. Take my yoke upon you and learn from me, for I am gentle and lowly in heart, and you will find rest for your souls. For my yoke is easy and my burden is light" (*Mt* 11:28-30).

While he was preaching, too, Christ had focused on the heart: "Blessed are the pure in heart, for they shall see God" (*Mt* 5:8). He also spoke of how for those who believed in him, his heart would become a fountain from which rivers of living water would flow (*Jn* 7:37-39). As St John goes on to point out, this was a reference to the Holy Spirit, who would be Christ's gift to his followers once he had been glorified.

Why did Christ focus in this way on the heart, both his own and that of others? Surely because the heart is universally recognised as the seat of the emotions, of human love. Although Jesus is God he is also man, and since the Incarnation, since his taking human flesh in the womb of the Blessed Virgin at the Annunciation, he has had a real human body and a real human heart.

So in the devotion to Christ's Sacred Heart we have a way of expressing our particular love for him as a real person, and not just an abstract religious figure. And since he lives forever to intercede for us, he reciprocates our love in an infinite way.

The growth of the devotion in the Middle Ages

The devotion to Christ's Sacred Heart can be traced back in a general way to the New Testament, as, for example, in the writings of St Paul and St John the Evangelist, with their focus on Christ's love for mankind. But it was only around the eleventh and twelfth centuries that this devotion really began to develop, particularly in Benedictine and Cistercian monasteries. Meditation on the wounded side of Christ ultimately led to a focus on his wounded heart. Certainly this devotion was well known to figures such as St Bernard, (1090-1153), St Bonaventure, (1221-1274), St Mechtilde, (1240/1241-1298) and St Gertrude (1256-1302).

Indeed, it is related that St Gertrude, who was a Benedictine nun, had a mystical experience on the feast of St John the Evangelist, in which she rested her head near the wound in Christ's side and heard the beating of his heart. She asked St John, who was also present, why he had never spoken of this in his Gospel, and he told her that this new revelation was reserved for those times when love for God in the world, having grown cold, would need to be rekindled.

Between the thirteenth and sixteenth centuries, this devotion was practised in a private way by many people, and also in a number of religious congregations. Various prayers and exercises were recommended for the devotion, as can be seen in the works of writers such as John of Avila

(1499-1569), Louis of Blois (1506-1566) and, later on, St Francis de Sales (1567-1622), particularly in his *Treatise on the Love of God*.

St John Eudes and the Sacred Heart devotion

From this point on, the Sacred Heart devotion flourished, being practised by many Jesuits, including St Francis Borgia and St Peter Canisius. It was also popular amongst some Carmelites and Benedictines, and particularly in the Visitation Order founded in 1610 by St Jane Frances de Chantal and St Francis de Sales for those women who did not have the physical strength to undergo the regime then current in other religious orders.

It was St John Eudes (1602-1680), however, a French missionary and founder of two religious orders, who elevated the status of the devotion by composing an office and establishing a feast for the Sacred Heart. Interestingly, he began by promoting devotion to the Heart of Mary, and only later did he focus on devotion to the Sacred Heart. These two devotions, and particularly the devotion to the Sacred Heart, acted as a spiritual antidote to the increasing rationalism of European society during this period. It was also around this time that Jansenism, a Calvinist-influenced strain of teaching, was causing a "coldness" to enter into Catholic life in France.

St John Eudes was instrumental in promoting the first feast of the Sacred Heart of Jesus in 1670, at Rennes in

France. This devotion spread to other dioceses and was adopted by various religious communities, eventually coalescing with that which originated through the work of St Margaret Mary Alacoque (1647-1690).

The first and second apparitions to St Margaret Mary

Margaret Mary was a religious of the Visitation Order who had been attracted to this order because of her delicate health. Christ appeared to her on a number of occasions with revelations about the love of his Sacred Heart for mankind. Like St Gertrude, she was given the privilege of resting her head upon Christ's Heart, and being told how much he loved mankind and sought a return for this love. This particular revelation occurred on 27th December, the feast of St John the Evangelist, probably in 1673, while Margaret Mary was a nun in the Visitation convent at Paray-le-Monial, a small town in the Burgundy region of eastern France.

She related what happened to Fr Claude de la Colombière, who was in charge of the Jesuit house in the town, describing how she had a vision of Jesus, during which she was given some idea of the greatness of his love for mankind. She also related how Christ told her that he wanted her to announce this love. A similar theme was expressed during the second apparition, early in 1674, when Margaret Mary saw Jesus' Sacred Heart on a throne of flames, transparent as crystal, surrounded by a crown of thorns signifying the sins of mankind, with a cross above it. Again Jesus told her of his infinite love for mankind and his desire that he should be honoured through the display of this image of his heart, with the promise that all who did so would be especially blessed. This vision is the origin of the traditional Sacred Heart picture which became so well known in later centuries, as indicated in one of the promises made by Christ to her: "I will bless every place where a picture of my Sacred Heart shall be exposed and honoured."

The third and fourth apparitions to St Margaret Mary

The third apparition probably took place on 2nd July 1674, while Margaret Mary was praying before the Blessed Sacrament. She saw a vision of Jesus in glory, with his five wounds shining like suns. He then showed her his heart on fire with love for mankind, a love that was often ignored or treated with contempt. He asked her to make up for this coldness and ingratitude by receiving Holy Communion as often as she was allowed, and particularly on the first Friday of each month.

The fourth apparition, which probably took place on 16th June 1675, was the most important. As before, it happened as Margaret Mary was praying before the Blessed Sacrament. Jesus again showed her a representation of his heart, further complaining of the ingratitude and coldness of mankind towards him, and particularly those specially consecrated to him. To make up for this he asked that the first Friday after the feast of Corpus Christi should be dedicated as a feast in honour of his Sacred Heart, and become an occasion for the faithful to receive Holy Communion in reparation.

The great promise of the Sacred Heart

The "great promise" associated with this devotion applies to those who go to Communion on nine consecutive First Fridays: "I promise you, in the excess of the mercy of my Heart, that its all-powerful love will grant to all those who shall receive Communion on the first Friday of nine consecutive months the grace of final repentance; they shall not die under my displeasure nor without receiving the Sacraments, my divine Heart becoming their assured refuge at that last hour."

To qualify for this tremendous grace, it is necessary to receive Holy Communion validly and worthily, that is, not being in a state of mortal sin, on the nine consecutive First Fridays as stated. In addition, the communicant must have the intention, at least implicitly, of making reparation to the Sacred Heart of Jesus for all the sins and ingratitude of mankind.

This series of apparitions has been approved by the Church, which has vouched for their authenticity, as far as is possible: the writings of Margaret Mary, which included these revelations and her letters, were examined during the process of her beatification, and their reliability is shown by the fact that they did not hinder her cause. Various popes, too, have expressed their approval of these apparitions, with their essential content being included in the bull of canonisation issued by Pope Benedict XV in 1920. And the feast of the Sacred Heart has been established in the Church calendar as requested.

Sacred Heart devotion and reparation

This devotion, then, is important in itself, but also because it exemplifies a theme, that of the need for repentance, for reparation, which has been central to the preaching of Christianity from the time of the apostles onwards: "Repent, for the kingdom of heaven is at hand" (*Mt* 3:2). The idea of making reparation, both for our own sins and, because of a common membership of the mystical body of Christ, for those of others, is only an extension of this basic Gospel message. As St Paul said: "Now I rejoice in my sufferings for your sake, and in my flesh I complete what is lacking in Christ's afflictions for the sake of his body, that is, the church ..." (*Col* 1:24).

The Sacred Heart devotion is really a reiteration of two thousand years of Christian teaching on the nature of Christ as both God and man. It is a refocusing on this fundamental point - that it was by the Incarnation and all that flowed from it, and particularly through the death and resurrection of Christ, that God has communicated his love to us in a most wonderful way, and that the gap between the infinity and holiness of God and the mortality and sinfulness of mankind has been bridged. Because Christ had a truly human heart, he can sympathise with us and understands all our needs, worries and sufferings "from the inside", because he too had a human nature capable of suffering.

The spread of the devotion

Shortly after the last apparition, Margaret Mary spoke to Fr de la Colombière, and as a result he was moved to consecrate himself to the Sacred Heart. He asked her to write an account of what had happened, and he then did what he could to make all this known both in France and in England, where he lived for three years.

After the death of Margaret Mary, in 1690, the devotion spread slowly but steadily, particularly in southern France; and in 1765 the Holy See allowed a feast of the Sacred Heart to be celebrated in the country as a whole. At the urging of the French bishops, in 1856, it was extended to the whole Church by Pope Pius IX, and it became a first class feast in 1889.

At the same time, acts of consecration and reparation to the Sacred Heart became increasingly popular throughout the Church, culminating in Pope Leo XIII's consecration of the world to the Sacred Heart in 1899. During the last third of the nineteenth century, various petitions advocating this had been addressed to the Holy See, but only after close study of the question did the Pope decide to carry out this act. That it was not a mere pious formality is shown by the fact that Pope Leo saw this as the "great act" of his pontificate. In the accompanying encyclical, *Annum Sacrum*, he justified his action on the basis that Christ, as son of God and Redeemer of humanity, had both natural and acquired rights over mankind. Therefore the consecration made sense as a further dedication of the human race to Christ, with his Sacred Heart as a tangible sign of his infinite love.

The devotion in recent history

In the meantime, the Visitation Convent at Paray-le-Monial developed as a shrine devoted to the Sacred Heart, and now up to 500,000 pilgrims each year come to visit the convent and the eleventh century Romanesque Basilica of the Sacred Heart in the town. Other shrines dedicated to this devotion have also been built. One of the best known of these is Sacré-Cœur Basilica, or the Basilica of the Sacred Heart, which is located on Montmartre in Paris, the place traditionally associated with the martyrdom of the first Bishop of Paris, St Denis, and his companions, in the late third century. At the time of the Franco-Prussian war in 1870, the idea of building a church consecrated to the Sacred Heart, in reparation for the sins of the French nation, gained support. Construction of the Romano-

Byzantine edifice, modelled on the chirches of Saint Sophia in Constantinople and St Mark in Venice, began in 1874, but the building was not finished until 1914, while its consecration was delayed until after World War I.

In England, Maryvale House in Birmingham has a chapel in which is housed what became, in the early nineteenth century, the first public Shrine of the Sacred Heart in the country. This was initiated by Bishop Milner, the Vicar Apostolic of the Midland District. He was deeply devoted to the Sacred Heart and when the main chapel in the house was being expanded, he built a small chapel above the sacristy to act as a shrine to the Sacred Heart. He had brought back from Rome a panel of painted glass which depicted the Sacred Heart of Jesus, as described by Saint Gertrude, and this was installed in the chapel as a way of promoting the devotion.

The popes on Sacred Heart devotion

Popes Pius XI and Pius XII on Sacred Heart devotion

In his encyclical on reparation to the Sacred Heart, *Miserentissimus Redemptor*, published in 1928, Pope Pius XI stated that:

> "There is surely no reason for doubting, Venerable Brethren, that from this devotion piously established and commanded to the whole Church, many excellent

benefits will flow forth, not only to individual men, but also to society, sacred, civil and domestic, seeing that our Redeemer himself promised to Margaret Mary that 'all those who rendered this honour to his Heart would be endowed with an abundance of heavenly graces'."

In 1956 the next Pope, Pius XII, likewise published an encyclical on this topic, entitled *Haurietis Aquas*, with the intention of promoting devotion to the Sacred Heart. In this he wrote:

> "It is altogether impossible to enumerate the heavenly gifts which devotion to the Sacred Heart of Jesus has poured out on the souls of the faithful, purifying them, offering them heavenly strength, rousing them to the attainment of all virtues. We are perfectly justified in seeing in this same devotion, which flourishes with increasing fervour throughout the world, a gift without price which our divine Saviour the Incarnate Word, as the one mediator of grace and truth between the heavenly father and the human race, imparted to the Church, his mystical Spouse, in recent centuries when she had to endure such trials and surmount so many difficulties."

Popes John Paul II and Benedict XVI on Sacred Heart devotion

On 24th June 2002, St Pope John Paul II spoke of this devotion at an Angelus address in St Peter's Square as follows:

> "To celebrate the Heart of Christ means to go to the inner centre of the person of the Saviour, the centre which the Bible identifies as his Heart, the seat of the love that has redeemed the world. If the human heart is really an unfathomable mystery known only to God, how much more sublime is the Heart of Jesus in whom the very life of the Word is pulsating. Echoing the Scriptures, the beautiful Litany of the Sacred Heart suggests that we find in the Heart of Jesus all the treasures of wisdom and knowledge and the whole fullness of divinity. To save man, the victim of his own disobedience, God wanted to give him a 'new heart' that would be faithful to his loving will. This heart is the Heart of Jesus, the Holy Spirit's masterpiece, which began to beat in Mary's virginal womb and was pierced by the spear as Jesus hung on the cross, becoming for all an inexhaustible source of eternal life. That Heart is now a pledge of hope for every man and woman."

More recently, Pope Benedict XVI, in a letter dated May 2006, wrote to the Superior General of the Jesuits on the 50th anniversary of Pope Pius's encyclical, stating:

> "By encouraging devotion to the Heart of Jesus, the Encyclical *Haurietis Aquas* exhorted believers to open themselves to the mystery of God and of his love, and to allow themselves to be transformed by it. After 50 years, it is still a fitting task for Christians to continue to deepen their relationship with the Heart of Jesus, in such a way as to revive their faith in the saving love of God and to welcome him ever more fully into their lives."

Pope Francis on the Sacred Heart devotion

Pope Francis, a Jesuit, has also been keen to promote devotion to the Sacred Heart. In his 9th June 2013 Angelus address at the Vatican, he said:

> "The month of June is traditionally dedicated to the Sacred Heart of Jesus, the highest human expression of divine love. Just this past Friday, in fact, we celebrated the Solemnity of the Sacred Heart of Jesus: the feast that sets the tone for the whole month. Popular piety highly prizes symbols, and the Heart of Jesus is the ultimate symbol of God's mercy - but it is not an imaginary symbol, it is a real symbol, which represents the centre, the source from which salvation for all humanity gushed forth... The Lord is always watching us with mercy, always awaits us with mercy. Let us be not afraid to approach him! He has a merciful heart! If we show our inner wounds, our sins, he always forgives us. He is pure mercy! Let us never forget this: He is pure mercy! Let us go to Jesus!"

Prayers and devotions to be said before the statue/icon

Our Lord's twelve promises to St Margaret Mary

The promises will become operative in the lives of those who honour the Sacred Heart by undertaking a novena of nine Holy Communions on nine successive first Fridays of the month, with the right dispositions, and especially with the intention of making reparation to the Heart of Jesus for one's own sins and sins committed by others:

I will give them all the graces necessary for their state of life.

I will establish peace in their homes.

I will comfort them in all their afflictions.

I will be their secure refuge during life, and especially at the hour of death.

I will bestow abundant blessings on all their undertakings.

Sinners shall find in my Heart the source and ocean of infinite mercy.

Tepid souls shall become fervent.

Fervent souls shall rise rapidly to a high degree of perfection.

I will bless every place where a picture of my Sacred Heart shall be exposed and honoured.

I will give to priests the power to touch the hardest hearts.

Those who shall promote this devotion shall have their names written in my Heart, never to be blotted out.

I promise you, in the excessive mercy of my Heart, that its all-powerful love will grant to all those who receive Holy Communion on the First Friday of every month for nine consecutive months, the grace of final repentance, and that they shall not die without receiving the sacraments, and that my Divine Heart shall be their safe refuge in that last moment.

Daily prayers

Prayer on awakening

I adore, praise, and salute you, O most sweet Heart of Jesus Christ. I thank you for having preserved me during this night, and for having rendered to God the Father praises and thanksgivings on my behalf. And now I offer you my heart as a morning sacrifice; I place it in your most tender Heart and entrust it to your keeping; deign to pour into it your divine inspiration, and to enkindle it with your holy love. Amen.

(St Gertrude, d. 1302)

Morning offering

O Jesus, through the most pure heart of Mary, I offer you all the prayers, works and sufferings of this day for all the intentions of your divine Heart.

O most Sacred Heart of Jesus, I place all my trust in thee (*three times*). Amen.

For a happy death

Remember, O Lord, the words which you spoke on the cross: "Father, into your hands I commend my spirit." I pray you receive my soul, when it must leave my sinful body, into the loving wound of your Heart. O dear Lord Jesus Christ, remember how on the cross your blessed Heart broke in the bitterness of death. When in my last hour my heart shall break in death, give me, I beseech you, this grace, that you may find in my soul perfect love, true contrition, firm faith, and unshakable trust in your mercy. Amen.

(Marienvrede, Convent of the Cross)

Evening prayer

O good and merciful God, I thank you for keeping me this day in life and health, as also for all the good things you have given me, for body and soul, for time and eternity. I offer and commend to your holy Heart any good thing that I have by your kindness today thought, spoke, and done, and all that I have had to bear of cross and suffering. I pray you to unite them to the love of your holy Heart, to your bitter Passion, and your merits, that they may please you and profit me to eternal life. Amen.

(From an unknown medieval author)

A prayer for the whole world

Out of his infinite glory, may God give you the power through his Spirit for your hidden self to grow strong, so that Christ may live in your hearts through faith, and then, planted in love and built on love, you will with all the Saints have strength to grasp the breadth and the length, the height and the depth; until knowing the love of Christ, which is beyond all knowledge, you are filled with the utter fullness of God. (*Ep* 3:16-19)

Readings and Collect from Feast of Sacred Heart, Year A

Collect

Grant, we pray, almighty God,
that we, who glory in the Heart
of your beloved Son

and recall the wonders of his love for us,
may be made worthy to receive
an overflowing measure of grace
from that fount of heavenly gifts.
Through our Lord Jesus Christ,
your Son, who lives and reigns with you in the
unity of the Holy Spirit,
one God, for ever and ever.

First reading - Deuteronomy 7:6-11

Moses said to the people: 'You are a people consecrated to the Lord your God; it is you that the Lord your God has chosen to be his very own people out of all the peoples on the earth. If the Lord set his heart on you and chose you, it was not because you outnumbered other peoples: you were the least of all peoples. It was for love of you and to keep the oath he swore to your fathers that the Lord brought you out with his mighty hand and redeemed you from the house of slavery, from the power of Pharaoh king of Egypt. Know then that the Lord your God is God indeed, the faithful God who is true to his covenant and his graciousness for a thousand generations towards those who love him and keep his commandments, but who punishes in their own persons those that hate him; he makes him work out his punishment in person. You are therefore to keep and observe the commandments and statutes and ordinances that I lay down for you today.'

Second reading - The first Letter of St John, 4:7-16

My dear people,
let us love one another
since love comes from God
and everyone who loves is begotten by God
  and knows God.
Anyone who fails to love can never have known God,
because God is love.
God's love for us was revealed
when God sent into the world his only Son
so that we could have life through him;
this is the love I mean:
not our love for God,
but God's love for us when he sent his Son
to be the sacrifice that takes our sins away.
My dear people,
since God has loved us so much,
we too should love one another.
no one has ever seen God;
but as long as we love one another
God will live in us
and his love will be complete in us.
We can know that we are living in him
and he is living in us
because he lets us share his Spirit.
We ourselves saw and we testify

that the Father sent his Son
as saviour of the world.
If anyone acknowledges that Jesus is the Son of God,
God lives in him, and he in God.
We ourselves have known and put our faith in
God's love towards ourselves.
God is love
and anyone who lives in love lives in God,
and God lives in him.

Gospel - Matthew 11:25-30

Jesus exclaimed, "I bless you, Father, lord of heaven and of earth, for hiding these things from the learned and the clever and revealing them to mere children. Yes, Father, for that is what it pleased you to do. Everything has been entrusted to me by my Father; and no one knows the Son except the Father, just as no one knows the Father except the Son and those to whom the Son chooses to reveal him."

"Come to me, all you who labour and are overburdened, and I will give you rest. Shoulder my yoke and learn from me, for I am gentle and humble in heart, and you will find rest for your souls. Yes, my yoke is easy and my burden light."

Litany of the Sacred Heart

Lord, have Mercy; *Lord, have Mercy*
Christ, have Mercy; *Christ, have Mercy*
Lord, have Mercy; *Lord, have Mercy*
God the Father in Heaven, *have Mercy on us*
(*"Have Mercy on us" is repeated after each invocation*)
God the Son, Redeemer of the world,
God the Holy Spirit,
Holy Trinity, one God,
Heart of Jesus, Son of the Eternal Father,
Heart of Jesus, Formed in the womb
of the Virgin Mother,
Heart of Jesus, One with the Eternal Word,
Heart of Jesus, Infinite in Majesty,
Heart of Jesus, Holy Temple of God,
Heart of Jesus, Tabernacle of the Most High,
Heart of Jesus, House of God and Gate of Heaven,
Heart of Jesus, Aflame with love for us,
Heart of Jesus, Source of Justice and Love,
Heart of Jesus, Full of Goodness and Love,
Heart of Jesus, Wellspring of all Virtue,
Heart of Jesus, Worthy of all praise,
Heart of Jesus, King and Centre of all hearts,
Heart of Jesus, Treasure-house of Wisdom
and Knowledge,
Heart of Jesus, In Whom dwells the fullness of God,

Heart of Jesus, In whom the Father is well pleased,
Heart of Jesus,
From Whose fullness we have all received,
Heart of Jesus, Desire of the Eternal Hills,
Heart of Jesus, Patient and full of Mercy,
Heart of Jesus, Generous to all who turn to You,
Heart of Jesus, Fountain of Life and Holiness,
Heart of Jesus, Atonement for our sins,
Heart of Jesus, Obedient even to death,
Heart of Jesus, Pierced by a lance,
Heart of Jesus, Source of all Consolation,
Heart of Jesus, Our Life and Resurrection,
Heart of Jesus, Our Peace and Reconciliation,
Heart of Jesus, Victim for our sins,
Heart of Jesus, Salvation of all who trust in You,
Heart of Jesus, Hope of all who die in You,
Heart of Jesus, Delight of all the Saints,
Lamb of God, You take away the sins of the world,
Spare us, O Lord.
Lamb of God, You take away the sins of the world,
Graciously hear us, O Lord.
Lamb of God, You take away the sins of the world,
Have Mercy on us.

V. Jesus, meek and humble of heart.
R. *Make our hearts like unto Thine.*

Let us pray:

Father, we rejoice in the gifts of love we have received from the Heart of Jesus, your Son. Open our hearts to share his Life and continue to bless us with his Love. We ask this in the name of Jesus the Lord. Amen.

Prayer of St Margaret Mary Alacoque

Lord Jesus, let my heart never rest until it finds you, who are its centre, its love, and its happiness.
By the wound in your Heart
pardon the sins that I have committed
whether out of malice or out of evil desires.
Place my weak heart in your own divine Heart,
continually under your protection and guidance,
so that I may persevere in doing good
and in fleeing evil until my last breath. Amen.

Prayer to the Sacred Heart by St Margaret Mary

Hail, Heart of Jesus, save me!
Hail, Heart of my Creator, perfect me!
Hail, Heart of my Saviour, deliver me!
Hail, Heart of my Judge, grant me pardon!
Hail, Heart of my Father, govern me!
Hail, Heart of my Spouse, grant me love!
Hail, Heart of my Master, teach me!
Hail, Heart of my King, be my crown!
Hail, Heart of my Benefactor, enrich me!

Hail, Heart of my Shepherd, guard me!
Hail, Heart of my Friend, comfort me!
Hail, Heart of my Brother, stay with me!
Hail, Heart of the Child Jesus, draw me to Yourself!
Hail, Heart of Jesus dying on the Cross, redeem me!
Hail, Heart of Jesus in all Your states,
give Yourself to me!
Hail, Heart of incomparable goodness,
have mercy on me!
Hail, Heart of splendour, shine within me!
Hail, most loving Heart, inflame me!
Hail, most merciful Heart, work within me!
Hail, most humble Heart, dwell within me!
Hail, most patient Heart, support me!
Hail, most faithful Heart, be my reward!
Hail, most admirable and most worthy Heart, bless me!

Acts of reparation

Act of reparation to the Mystical Body

Lord Jesus Christ, we look at the cross, and we, your pilgrim Church, can see what sin has done to the son of Mary, to the Son of God. But now you are risen and glorified. You suffer no more in the flesh. Sin can no longer expose you to the Agony in the Garden, to the scourging, to the death on a cross. But it can reach you through your Mystical Body.

This is part of you. Your Church on earth still feels the strength of sin. For this we make our act of reparation. We, who have sinned in the past, now consecrate ourselves to the healing of your Mystical Body. Sanctify us for this task. May your Sacred Heart be the symbol, not of one love, but of two. Your love for us and our love for you. Accept our love and help us make it real by serving you in all our brothers and sisters, so that love and concern may lead all people to know the one true God and Jesus Christ whom he has sent. Amen.

Act of reparation to the Most Sacred Heart of Jesus

Most sweet Jesus, whose overflowing charity for men is requited by so much forgetfulness, negligence and contempt, behold us prostrate before you, eager to repair by a special act of homage the cruel indifference and injuries to which your loving Heart is everywhere subject.

Mindful, alas! that we ourselves have had a share in such great indignities, which we now deplore from the depths of our hearts, we humbly ask your pardon and declare our readiness to atone by voluntary expiation, not only for our own personal offences, but also for the sins of those, who, straying far from the path of salvation, refuse in their obstinate infidelity to follow you, their Shepherd and Leader, or, renouncing the promises of their baptism, have cast off the sweet yoke of your law. We are now resolved to expiate each and every deplorable outrage committed against you; we are now determined to make amends for the manifold offences against Christian modesty in unbecoming dress and behaviour, for all the foul seductions laid to ensnare the feet of the innocent, for the frequent violations of Sundays and holydays, and the shocking blasphemies uttered against you and your Saints.

We wish also to make amends for the insults to which your Vicar on earth and your priests are subjected, for the profanation, by conscious neglect or terrible acts of sacrilege, of the very Sacrament of your divine love, and lastly for the public crimes of nations who resist the rights and teaching authority of the Church which you have founded. Would that we were able to wash away such abominations with our blood.

We now offer, in reparation for these violations of your divine honour, the satisfaction you once made to your Eternal Father on the cross and which you continue to renew daily on our altars; we offer it in union with the acts of atonement of your Virgin Mother and all the Saints and of the pious faithful on earth; and we sincerely promise to make recompense, as far as we can with the help of your grace, for all neglect of your great love and for the sins we and others have committed in the past.

Henceforth, we will live a life of unswerving faith, of purity of conduct, of perfect observance of the precepts of the Gospel and especially that of charity. We promise to the best of our power to prevent others from offending you and to bring as many as possible to follow you.

O loving Jesus, through the intercession of the Blessed Virgin Mother, our model in reparation, deign to receive the voluntary offering we make of this act of expiation; and by the crowning gift of perseverance keep us faithful unto death in our duty and the allegiance we owe to you, so that we may all one day come to that happy home, where with the Father and the Holy Spirit you live and reign, God, for ever and ever. Amen.

(*A partial indulgence is granted to the faithful who piously recite the above act of reparation. A plenary indulgence is granted if it is publicly recited on the feast of the Most Sacred Heart of Jesus.*)

Meditations

"We too, pilgrims in the flesh, love as much as we can, and embrace the One who was wounded for us, whose hands, feet, side and Heart were pierced. Let us love and pray: 'O Jesus, deign to bind our hearts, still so hard and unrepentant, with the chain of your love and wound them with its dart.' "

(St Bonaventure)

"O Jesus, a soldier opened your side with his lance, so that, through the gaping wound, we might know the charity of your Heart, which loved us unto death, and that we might enter into your unutterable love through the same channel by which it came to us. Approach, then, O my soul, the Heart of Christ, that magnanimous Heart, that hidden Heart, that Heart which thinks of all things and knows all things; that loving Heart, all on fire with love. Make me understand, O Lord, that the door of your Heart was forced open by the vehemence of your love. Allow me to enter into the secret of that love which was hidden from all eternity, but is now revealed by the wound in your Heart."

(St Bernadine of Siena)

Meditation by St John Eudes

The most loving heart of our benign Saviour is a burning furnace of most pure love for us; a furnace of purifying love, of illuminating love, of sanctifying love, of transforming love and of deifying love. His love is a purifying love, in which the hearts of holy souls are purified more perfectly than gold in the furnace; an illuminating love, which scatters the darkness of hell with which the earth is covered and lets us into the wonderful brilliance of heaven: "who has called you out of darkness into his marvellous light (1 *P* 2:9); a sanctifying love, which destroys sin in our souls in order to establish there the kingdom of grace; a transforming love, which transforms serpents into doves, wolves into lambs, beasts into angels, children of the devil into children of God, children of wrath and malediction into children of grace and blessing; a deifying love, which makes gods of men: "I have said: you are gods" (*Ps* 82:6), letting them share in the holiness of God, his mercy, his patience, his goodness, his love, his charity and his other divine perfections: "Partakers of the divine nature" (2 *P* 1:4). O divine love of my Jesus, I give myself wholly to you; purify me, enlighten me, sanctify me, transform me into you, that I may be naught but love for my God.

Meditation by Cardinal Newman

O most sacred, most loving Heart of Jesus, Thou art concealed in the Holy Eucharist, and Thou beatest for us still. Now as then Thou sayest, "With desire I have desired." I worship Thee, then, with all my best love and awe, with my fervent affection, with my most subdued, most resolved will. O make my heart beat with Thy heart. Purify it of all that is earthly, all that is proud and sensual, all that is hard and cruel, of all perversity, of all disorder, of all deadness. So fill it with Thee, that neither the events of the day nor the circumstances of the time may have power to ruffle it; but that in Thy love and Thy fear it may have peace.

Meditation on devotion to the Sacred Heart

Devotion to the Heart of our Divine Lord may be said to be the highest and most complete form of homage to his Sacred Humanity, inasmuch as it involves not only the worship of his material heart of flesh, but moreover, in a special manner, the worship of that divine love incarnate in his heart, which was the spring of every word and action of his life. Hence it is to the Heart of Our Blessed Lord, that are to be traced all those marvellous lessons of humility, submission, charity, and all other virtues of which his whole mortal career affords us so brilliant an illustration. In studying that heart, the great mystery of the Incarnation becomes clearer to us, and the means chosen by the Eternal for the redemption of the world, and manifested in Our Lord Jesus Christ, break on us in a new light, indicating at the same time the only means by which society in the present day, the nations, the whole world, will find salvation from the evils that threaten the destruction of authority, of legitimate government, of subordination, both civil and religious - in a word, of all order, social and divine.

What then, are the tendencies characterising the devotion to the Heart of the Incarnate God? Before, and above all, submission. "*Descendit de caelis… et homo factus est.*" ("He came down from heaven … and became man.") Such was the first lesson imparted to men by him who came to save them. He would teach them that the very foundation of all salvation should consist in and rest upon these two acknowledgements; the supreme sovereignty - the unlimited dominion of God, and, the absolute nothingness, and consequent utter dependence of the creature upon that infinite being who alone is. From thence would flow obedience to his laws, submission to those representing his authority, and lastly, a spirit of subordination to all legitimately instituted power, inasmuch and as far as it was in harmony with the order of God… If the sublime doctrine of the Heart of Jesus were more fully comprehended, and made to bear upon actual difficulties involving the gravest interests, how different an aspect would the world present at this hour.

(Fr Benedict Sestini SJ, d. 1890)

Meditation by St Thérèse of Lisieux

I need a heart burning with tenderness,
Who will be my support for ever,
Who loves everything in me, even my weakness…
And who never leaves me day or night.
I could find no creature
Who could always love me day or night.
I could find no creature
Who could always love me and never die.
I must have a God who takes on my nature
And becomes my brother and is able to suffer!
You heard me, only Friend whom I love.
To ravish my heart, you became man.
You shed Your blood, what a supreme mystery!
O Heart of Jesus, treasure of tenderness,
You Yourself are my happiness, my only hope.
You who knew how to charm my tender youth,
Stay near me till the last night…
Ah! I know well, all our righteousness
is worthless in your sight.

To give value to my sacrifices,
I want to cast them into Your Divine Heart.
You did not find Your angels without blemish.
In the midst of lightning You gave Your law!
I hide myself in Your Sacred Heart, Jesus.
I do not fear, my virtue is You!

Hymns

To Christ the Prince of Peace

To Christ the Prince of Peace,
And Son of God most high,
The Father of the world to come,
Sing we with holy joy.

Deep in His heart, for us,
The wound of love He bore;
That love wherewith He still inflames
The hearts that Him adore.

O Jesu, victim blest,
What else but love divine
Could Thee constrain to open thus
That Sacred Heart of thine?

O fount of endless life,
O spring of water clear,
O flame celestial, cleansing all
Who unto Thee draw near!

Hide us in Thy dear heart,
For thither do we fly;
There seek Thy grace through life; in death
Thine immortality.

Praise to the Father be,
And sole-begotten Son;
Praise, Holy Paraclete, to thee,
While endless ages run.

(*Catholicum Hymnologium Germanicum*
1587, Tr. E. Caswell, 1814-1878)

O Sacred Heart

O Sacred Heart,
our home lies deep in thee;
on earth thou art an exile's rest,
in heav'n the glory of the blest,
O Sacred Heart.

O Sacred Heart,
thou fount of contrite tears:
where'er those living waters flow,
new life to sinners they bestow,
O Sacred Heart.

O Sacred Heart,
our trust is all in thee,

for though earth's night be dark and drear,
thou breathest rest where thou art near,
O Sacred Heart.

O Sacred Heart,
when shades of death shall fall,
receive us 'neath thy gentle care,
and save us from the tempter's snare,
O Sacred Heart.

O Sacred Heart,
lead exiled children home,
where we may ever rest near thee,
in peace and joy eternally,
O Sacred Heart.

(Francis Stanfield, 1835-1914)

Sweet Heart of Jesus

Sweet Heart of Jesus fount of love and mercy,
Today we come Thy blessing to implore,
O touch our hearts so cold and so ungrateful,
And make them Lord Thine own for ever more.

Chorus
Sweet Heart of Jesus we Thee implore,
O make us love Thee, more and more.

Sweet heart of Jesus, make us know and love Thee,
Unfold to us the treasurers of Thy grace,
That so our hearts from things of earth uplifted,
May long alone, to gaze upon Thy face.

Sweet Heart of Jesus make us pure and gentle,
And teach us how to do Thy blessed Will,
To follow close the prints of Thy dear footsteps,
And when we fall, Sweet Jesus love us still.

Sweet Heart of Jesus bless all hearts that love Thee
And may Thine own Heart ever blessed be
Bless us dear Lord , and bless the friends we cherish
And keep us true to Mary and to Thee.

(Cited as "Author unknown"
in Hymns Old and New, Mayhew)

Prayers of consecration to the Sacred Heart

I give and consecrate to the Heart of our Lord Jesus Christ, my whole life, all my actions, my trials, my sufferings, devoting every portion of my being to loving, honouring, and glorifying him, to working for his love alone, renouncing with all my heart whatever may be displeasing to him. I take you, then, O Sacred Heart, for the one object of my love, the protector of my life, the pledge of my salvation, the remedy of my inconstancy, the redeemer of all my faults, and my sure refuge in the hour of death. O Heart of all goodness, be my justification before God the Father, and shield me from the effects of his just anger. O Heart, overflowing with love, I place all my confidence in you, for I dread my own weakness, while I hope everything from your goodness. Destroy in me whatever displeases you or goes against your will. May pure love of you be so deeply imprinted in my heart that I may never forget you nor be separated from you. I implore you by all your love that my name may be graven upon you. May it be all my happiness to live and die as your slave. Amen.

(St Margaret Mary, d. 1690)

Act of consecration of St Claude de la Colombière

O adorable Saviour, vouchsafe my desire to consecrate myself entirely to the love and reparation of thy divine Heart and to accept the gift I make to thee of all that I am and all that I have. In reparation for all the outrages committed against thee and for the terrible ingratitude thou dost suffer from men, I consecrate to thee myself and my life. Give and take what thou wilt; use me or set me aside as a useless instrument; give me consolations or give me trials; may thy will be done in all things. May all this glorify thy divine Heart and make reparation to it. I wish to make a full gift of all this to thee, begging thee to accept it and use it freely for the salvation of sinners. Amen.

Consecration of the human race to the Sacred Heart

O most sweet Jesus, Redeemer of mankind, behold us humbly prostrate before your altar. We are yours, and yours we wish to be; and so that we may be united to you more closely, we consecrate ourselves to your most Sacred Heart. There are many who have never known you and many who have despised your teaching and rejected you. Have pity on them all most merciful Jesus and draw them to your Sacred Heart. Be King not only of the faithful who have never left you, but also of the prodigal children who have abandoned you. Let them return quickly to their Father's house lest they perish from misery and deprivation. Be King of those who have been misled by error or are divided from us by schism, and call them back to the haven of truth and unity of faith, that soon there may be one fold and one Shepherd. Grant to your Church, O Lord, safety and sure liberty; grant to all nations the peace that comes from order; and may all the earth resound from pole to pole with the one chant: Praise, honour and glory be forever to the Divine Heart which accomplished our salvation. Amen.

A novena for the First Fridays

Sacred Heart of Jesus, I unite myself:
To your adoration,
To your burning love,
To your ardent zeal,
To your reparation,
To your thanksgiving,
To your firm confidence,
To your fervent prayers,
To your silence,
To your humility,
To your obedience,
To your gentleness and peace,
To your surpassing kindness,
To your universal charity,
To your deep recollection,
To your intense desire for the conversion of sinners,
To your close union with the Heavenly Father,
To your intentions, desires, and will. Amen.

Love of the Heart of Jesus,
Inflame my heart.
Charity of the Heart of Jesus,
Abound in my heart.
Strength of the Heart of Jesus,
Uphold my heart.

Mercy of the Heart of Jesus,
Forgive my heart.
Patience of the Heart of Jesus,
Do not weary of my heart.
Kingdom of the Heart of Jesus,
Be established in my heart.
Wisdom of the Heart of Jesus,
Teach my heart.
Will of the Heart of Jesus,
Dispose of my heart.
Zeal of the Heart of Jesus,
Consume my heart.
O Mary, conceived without sin,
Pray for us to the Heart of Jesus.

Sweet Jesus, who, through your tender love for the Church your Spouse, opened to her the riches and unspeakable sweetness of your Sacred Heart, grant that our hearts may be enriched with the treasures it contains and replenished with its overflowing and unfailing delights. Amen.

Saint Joseph
Prayers & Devotions

Parish Dispenser

by Donal Anthony Foley

The statues and paintings in Catholic churches and chapels are an aid to prayer and devotion for everyone.

This booklet explains the origins of devotion to St Joseph, and his importance in our everyday life and on our journey of faith. The best loved litanies, novenas, devotions and hymns are included to encourage a prayerful visit to Jesus's foster-father and a mind and heart lifted up to God.

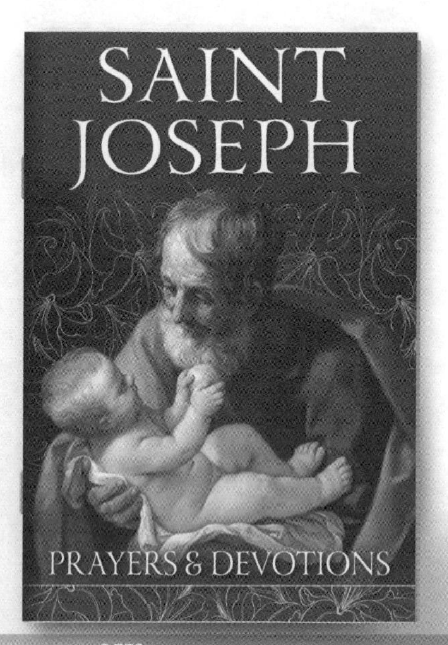

D772 ISBN 978 1 86082 910 9

Saint Thérèse of Lisieux
Prayers & Devotions

Parish Dispenser

by Donal Anthony Foley

The statues and paintings in Catholic churches and chapels are an aid to prayer and devotion for everyone.

This booklet contains an introduction to the life of St Therese and explains the origins of devotion to her and her importance in our everyday life and on our journey of faith. The best loved litanies, novenas, devotions and hymns are included to encourage a prayerful visit to this well loved Saint and Patroness of the Missions and a mind and heart lifted up to God.

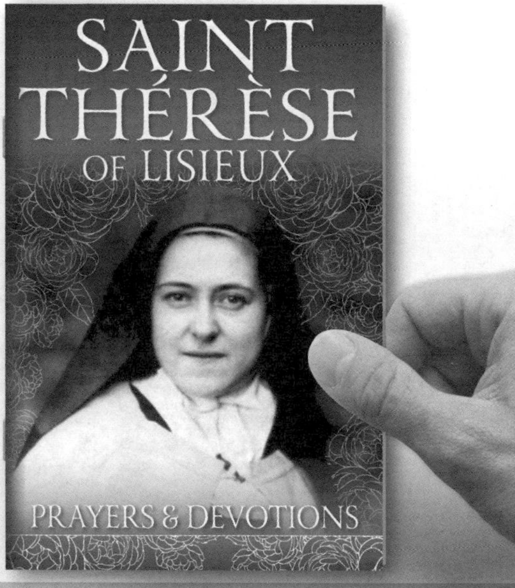

D771 ISBN 978 1 86082 909 3

The Sacred Heart
A Pilgrim's Companion to Paray-le-Monial

by David Baldwin

Set in the French shrine of Paray-le-Monial, this is the story of the devotion to the Sacred Heart, and of St Margaret Mary Alacoque and Saint Claude de la Colombiere in particular. It takes you to the principal pilgrim places of the modern genesis of this devotion, providing coherent commentary and narrative description, as well as suggesting appropriate prayers and meditations along the way.

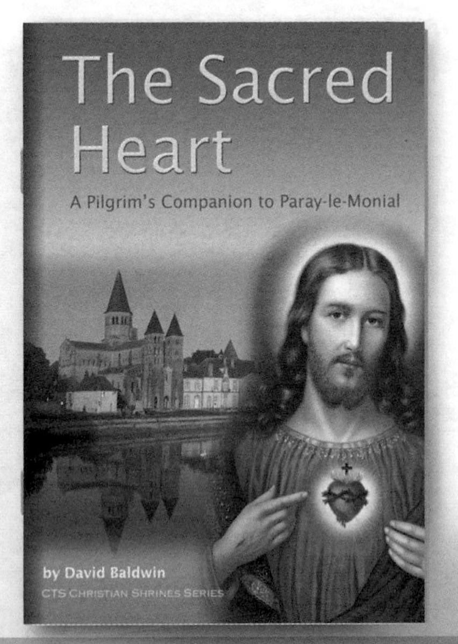

D718 ISBN 978 1 86082 628 3

Divine Mercy Prayer Book

by The Marian Fathers

The Divine Mercy message reminds us of what the Church has always taught: God is merciful and forgiving and we, too, must show mercy and forgiveness. It calls people to a deeper understanding that God's love is unlimited and available to everyone - especially the greatest sinners. Devotion to The Divine Mercy involves a total commitment to God as Mercy. The devotional practices proposed in the Diary of St Faustina and included here are completely in accordance with the teachings of the Church and firmly rooted in the Gospel message of our Merciful Saviour.

D725 ISBN 978 1 86082 637 5